I0115655

The CURLY COW

A TRUE STORY

JOANNE LE MAITRE

Published in Australia by Sid Harta Publishers Pty Ltd,
ABN: 46 119 415 842
23 Stirling Crescent, Glen Waverley, Victoria 3150 Australia
Telephone: +61 3 9560 9920, Facsimile: +61 3 9545 1742
E-mail: author@sidharta.com.au

First published in Australia 2018
This edition published 2018
Copyright © Joanne Le Maitre 2018
Cover design, typesetting: WorkingType (www.workingtype.com.au)

The right of Joanne Le Maitre to be identified as the Author of the Work has been asserted in accordance with the Copyright, Designs and Patents Act 1988.

All rights reserved. No part of this publication may be reproduced, stored in a retrieval system, or transmitted, in any form or by any means without the prior written permission of the publisher, nor be otherwise circulated in any form of binding or cover other than that in which it is published and without a similar condition being imposed on the subsequent purchaser.

Joanne Le Maitre
The Curly Cow
ISBN: 978-1-925230-36-9
pp38

ABOUT THE AUTHOR

Having spent most of her educational years in suburbia around the Newcastle region, Joanne Le Maitre became a farmer by default. After she graduated high school, her parents 'retired' onto a small property in the Hunter Valley. She took a job on a neighbouring property where she milked cows for a year before attending college. When an old brindle cow entered her life, it was here that her love affair with cattle began. After attending the local Agricultural College, she returned to the farm to dedicate her life to taking care of a herd of Murray Grey cattle and some Wiltshire Horn sheep. She still shares the farm with all her pets and wild friends.

PREFACE

This is a true story. Everything happened as described in the story about the love affair between an old jersey cow, her daughters and granddaughters, and the girl who looked after them. The story still goes on to this day, 37 years later.

Dedicated to my parents, without whose lifelong hard work, the privileged life that I lead with all the animals on my farm, both domestic and wild, would not have been possible. Thankyou.

CHAPTER 1

Grandma

Beaumont Pets Dream the 2nd lived on a small dairy farm at Knockfin in the Hunter Valley of New South Wales, and twice per day, every day, she gave her lovely creamy milk to the farmer who owned her. You may have guessed by now that Beaumont Pets Dream the 2nd was a dairy cow, a jersey cow more precisely, with a pair of mismatched horns and a lovely temperament.

Her registered name was a bit of a mouthful, so the farmer called her Seven Hills, after the place she was born on the 3rd of May, 1969.

In 1980, the elderly farmer decided to sell his farm and retire, so Seven Hills and all of her cow friends found themselves up for sale. Seven Hills had spent all of her working-life

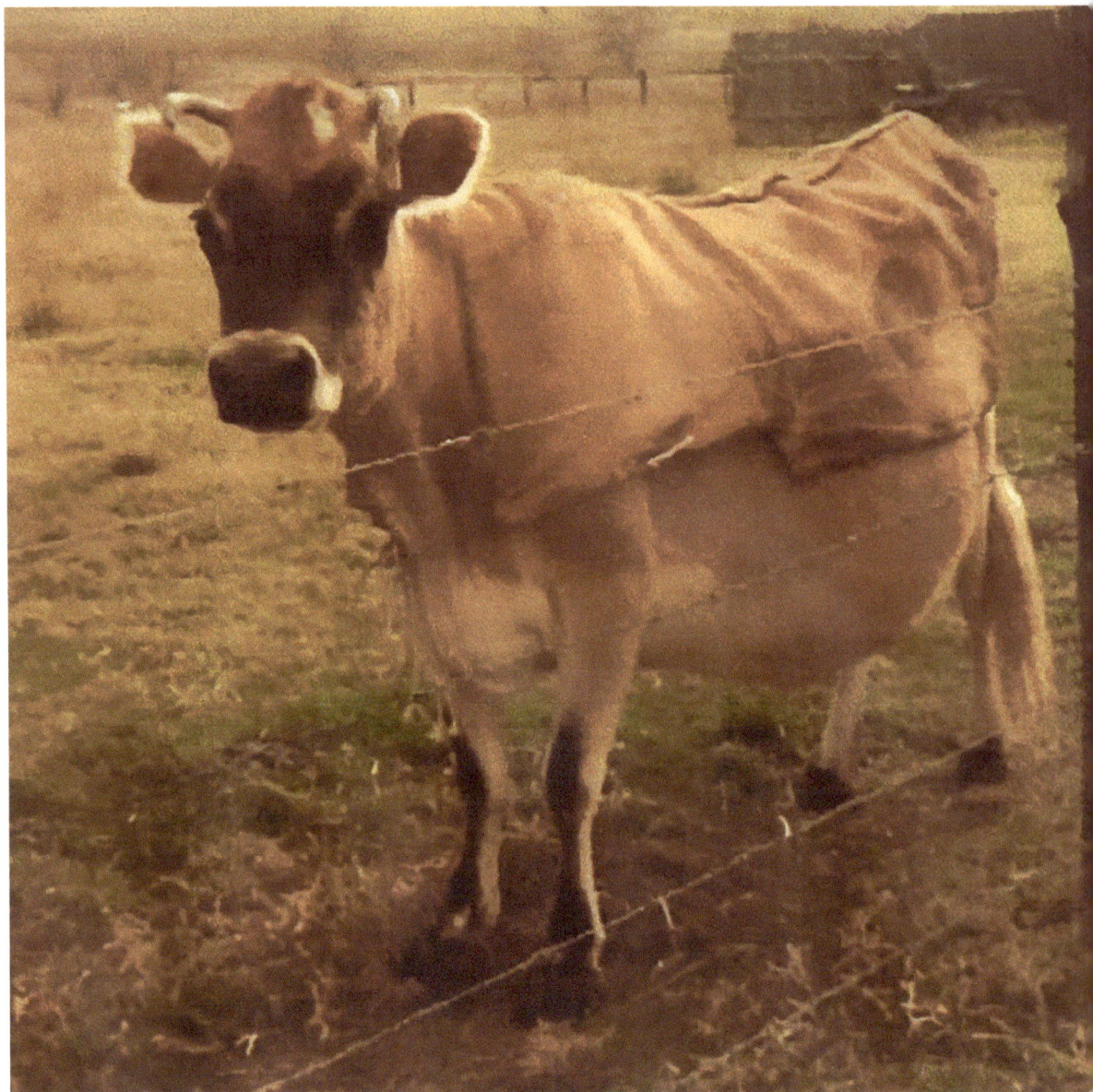

at the farm, and so it was quite an upheaval to be sold off to some stranger and go somewhere she did not know, with people she had never met. She was almost 11 years old, and for a dairy cow that is quite old, probably a little too old for another dairy farmer to want to buy her.

On the day of the sale, a kind-hearted man named George and his wife Winnie went to look at the cows because they had just moved onto a small farm themselves, with their daughter Joanne. George was not a farmer by trade but he decided to embrace country life and buy a house cow to milk.

George needed a quiet cow that was well behaved, and it didn't matter if she was a bit old, so when Seven Hills walked up to the fence where George and Winnie were standing, Seven Hills took a handful of grass straight out of George's hand. He decided that she was the cow for him and it was as if Seven Hills had just won the cow lottery!

The farmhand and his wife who had milked Seven Hills for all those years were pleased that she had gone to a good home, but they told George that she had only ever had bull calves, which was a shame because she was such a nice cow they had always wanted a heifer calf to keep as a replacement. Seven Hills was in-calf to a jersey bull when George bought her and shortly after arriving at her new home, she gave birth to another bull calf, who was named Caramello.

George, Winnie and Joanne had a small herd of Murray Grey cows on their farm, and so the next time that Seven (shortened from Seven Hills) went in-calf, it was to a Murray Grey bull named Glenalvon Huntsman.

CHAPTER 2

Shilling.

On the 26th March 1982, early in the morning on a lovely sunny day, old Seven gave birth to a black heifer calf. Joanne was beside herself with joy and excitement. She thought it was very special that Seven had given them her first heifer calf. The little calf was sleeping in the sun and on its black shiny coat, was a bird dropping. Joannes' grandma had a pet magpie that would come into the kitchen for something to eat, and when it pooped on the floor, grandma would say that he had done a shilling. A shilling was an old imperial coin about the size of a 10c piece, and magpie poop was about that size too. Shilling was a very inauspicious name for a calf that would start a dynasty, but she was named it anyway and was called 'Shill' for short.

CHAPTER 3

Milking.

When a cow lives on a dairy farm they don't get to keep their calves with them, because if they did, the farmer wouldn't get any milk. When George wanted to milk Seven for the house, he had to put young Shill in the calf shed overnight so that she didn't drink all of Seven's milk. Once he had milked enough for the house, about 3 litres every second day, young Shill got the rest. Even though the calf shed was warm and dry, and her Mum was right beside her in the shed, Shill didn't think much of this arrangement. She would bellow all night, or at least it seemed like all night when you were trying to sleep. Every now and then, Seven would bellow as well just for good measure.

Luckily George was an early riser, so Shill didn't have to wait too long for her breakfast. George would go out to the calf shed where Seven and Shill were waiting, and he would bring with him a bucket for the milk, a bucket of warm water with a wash cloth and a tin of dairy meal to feed Seven while he milked her. He would give Seven's udder a good wash with the warm water (no one would like to be washed with cold water on a cold morning) and then dry it off ready for milking. This ensured that the milk going into the bucket was free from any dirt or manure that Seven had laid in while resting in the paddock. He also aimed the first couple of squirts of milk onto the ground and not into the bucket for the same reason, as well as to check that Seven didn't have any mastitis, a bacterial infection which makes the milk go lumpy.

Once let out, Shill drank Seven dry, with copious bunting which means whacking her head against Seven's udder (which tells mum to let more milk down). Most people who don't milk cows don't realise that a cow can hold her milk up, and make it very hard for a calf or a dairy hand to get any milk out. Old Seven would always hold plenty of milk back for little Shill. When Shill finished her breakfast, she had a big white frothy beard around her mouth and nose, a mixture of milk and calf spit all in bubbles. Quite a sight, a black calf with a white frothy beard! Shill grew into a big cow on this rich diet.

CHAPTER 4

George's garden.

All the family loved old Seven, so one day when she was looking out of the verandah window, Joanne was surprised to see Seven in her paddock looking innocently at George who was vigorously wagging an index finger at her, like he was giving her a good telling off. And he was. Seven had discovered that if she tilted her head sideways and pushed, it would fit between the barbed wires on George's garden fence. She had just eaten most of the fine crop of green beans that George had taken weeks to grow, and she thought they were really yummy! Seven milked extra well the next morning, not because she was sorry about eating George' beans, but because nice green feed makes extra milk. Oh well, the family would have to make do with the

9

lovely homemade butter that Winnie made with the cream off Sevens' milk, or just enjoy the milk on their corn flakes. The cream was so yellow that it was almost orange, and so thick that you didn't have to whip it to put it on scones.

CHAPTER 5

Washing

Despite having oddly shaped horns, Seven was a pretty cow. She had a dark grey nose that was wet and sort of rubbery with a dimpled pattern in the skin, and around the edges where her nose met the rest of her face, the hairs grew in very short round patterns that reminded Joanne of the sundews that grew on the poor soil in the bush paddock of the property. Incidentally, the individual pattern on a cow's nose is like a human fingerprint, no two are the same, and you can identify a cow by its nose print. Her nose was surrounded by whitish hair of about one centimetre which then blended into a dark ginger colour and then into black. She had off-white eyebrows and a dark ginger forelock between her horns with a little patch of white hair on it. She also had a triangular white patch of hair on her left shoulder, and the rest of her was beautiful jersey gold, with black knee patches and socks. Her eyes were dark, dark brown and kind and her hooves were black.

She was so quiet that Joanne would take a bucket of warm soapy water out into the paddock with a dipper and a brush and give Seven a bath. Seven seemed to enjoy this attention and always loved being brushed. On hot dusty days in the summer, cows get dirt in their coats and get itchy, and besides, when Seven's white patches were washed, and the golden hair was free of dirt and sweat, she looked like Beaumont Pets Dream the 2nd again, the stud jersey cow.

On this particular day, a man was cleaning out a dam on the property near Seven's paddock with a bulldozer. He later told George that it was one of the funniest things he had ever seen, a cow being shampooed while just standing quietly in the paddock. What he didn't know was that when Joanne first came out to wash Seven, she was standing in the dairy shed chewing her cud in the shade. It was a hot summer day. Seven didn't want to move outside and Joanne didn't want to get the shed floor all wet, so she put the bucket of warm soapy water down just outside the shed and went to get a feed bin and some dairy meal to entice Seven to come outside. When Joanne came back with the

A painting of Seven done by Joanne.

feed, Seven was standing in exactly the same position in the shed and was still chewing her cud, but there was a big sloppy cow pat floating in Joanne's bucket of warm soapy water, and there were no other cattle in the paddock. Who could have guessed that cows have a sense of humour, or perhaps it was a subtle comment on what Seven really thought about getting washed. Joanne thought that beneath that calm cow exterior, Seven was probably laughing fit to split her sides. Joanne thought it was pretty funny too, but was not so easily deterred so she went and got more soapy water.

CHAPTER 6

Sirris

On the 3rd of September 1984 old Seven gave birth to a grey heifer calf, also sired by Huntsman. Everyone was thrilled, it seemed very special that Seven had given her new

family, two heifer calves to carry on her legacy. The new calf was named Sirris, because she looked just as good backwards as forwards.

Joanne was milking Seven for the house at the time, and consequently spent a lot of time with young Sirris. They became good friends, because Sirris was the most loving and gentle calf, always ready for a pat and cuddle, and she

remained like that all of her long life. She was destined how-ever to never have a calf of her own, unlike Shilling who had 15 calves over her lifetime, some who were very quiet like herself, and had remained at the small farm. George said to Joanne that she should sell Sirris because she was unable to have any calves and was not producing anything, but Joanne loved Sirris and would not do it. Sirris even outlived George, a fact that Joanne found ironic. Anyway, Sirris' finest moment was yet to come!

CHAPTER 7

A way of life

One morning in 1988, George was working near the dairy shed and he saw Seven walking along and then suddenly fall down. He thought she had slipped on the new concrete apron at the dairy shed that had been laid to stop the shed from getting wet and boggy in wet weather. Cows find it hard to walk on hard surfaces as their hooves sometimes slip, but the concrete had been finished roughly to help stop this from happening. Seven didn't seem to be able to get up, and George ran inside to get Joanne. Joanne called the vet immediately, and the lovely lady at the vet reception asked her if she was crying. She was. Joanne was distraught to think that something was wrong with her old friend, and even more so when the vet came and told her that Seven could not be saved. She had broken her shoulder bone, too high up to be set in plaster like a leg. Joanne would have paid anything to save her old friend, but nothing could be done. The vet told her that dairy cows put so much calcium into the milk that they make, that they get brittle bones when they get old, just like old people. Seven was buried in the paddock she lived in, and Joanne planted a silky oak tree on her grave that gave shade to the other animals that came after her.

As sad as Joanne was over losing Seven, she still had Shilling and Sirris to look after, as well as all the other animals on the farm. There was quite a menagerie, a cat named Tina, a topknot pigeon named Peep, a magpie named Squeaky Beak and a lot of Murray Grey cattle. Farmers can't call in sick when they have the flu or are just really, really sad. Their animals rely on them for their feed and water and wellbeing, so as trite as the old saying may seem, come rain, hail or shine, drought or flooding rain, in sickness and in health (yes, farmers are married to their job) they have to get out of bed even when they don't feel like it and do their work. As Joanne's Uncle Tobe says, "farming is not an occupation, it is a way of life."

CHAPTER 8

Chip

In 1990, Shilling gave birth to a grey bull calf who was so much like his sire that he was named Chip, (as in chip off the old block). On this particular morning, Joanne was milking Shilling and Chip was outside the dairy shed. George opened the gate to the paddock to drive the tractor and trailer through and Chip saw his opportunity to escape. He took off out the gate into the big paddock and flew outside like a rocket, tail in the air and legs pumping. He ran down the hill as fast as his legs could carry him and headed straight for the big dam at the bottom of the hill. The problem with this was that the dam was covered with duck weed, an aquatic plant that floats on top of the water and is varied in colour, from pale green to rusty red.

The soil and grass around the dam were also rusty red and green, and Chip couldn't tell the difference. He hit the water so hard and fast that there was an enormous splash, and Chip completely disappeared below the water. Joanne was starting to panic thinking the calf might drown and started running to the dam. After a few seconds which seemed much longer, two ears and the top of a head and nose appeared above the water, then there was a loud exhalation which made him spray water and duck weed out of his nose. Finally, Chip managed to negotiate his way to the bank where he climbed out onto dry land. A more forlorn sight you would not see. He stood with his head down coughing and spluttering, dripping with water and covered in duck weed. Even his ears had drooped, which happens when cows get water in their ears. Then he let out a loud mournful moo to his mother, trotted back up the hill and put himself back in his paddock and had a drink from Shilling which gave him comfort. He never tried to make a break for it again.

Shilling, calf and Sirris relaxing together.

CHAPTER 9

Zenith Shill

Of all the calves that Shilling had, only some were very quiet like her, but they all found a home for life. Sweet Pea, Snevel, Rastus and Sirris the 2nd all lived out their mostly long lives on the little farm. But Shilling saved the best for last. On the 12th of November 1998 she gave birth to a brindle heifer calf whose sire was a Wagyu bull named Itomichi. Joanne was thrilled, as her favourite colour for a cow was brindle which is a red and black striped coat that is very pretty. She was named Zenith Shill and registered in the appendix of the Wagyu registry.

A couple of weeks after the calf was born, Shilling was not herself. She was having trouble getting up and down in the paddock, and the vet said she had a type of arthritis. This got

worse in spite of treatment until Shilling couldn't get up at all one day and the vet said nothing else could be done. Joanne buried her in the paddock with her mum Seven Hills, and planted a peppercorn tree on her grave. Zenith Shill was only six weeks old when she lost her mum, so Joanne had to feed her on a bottle. The first afternoon that Shill was without her mum, Joanne sat with her in the shed so that the little calf wouldn't be lonely or afraid, she was calling for her mum but there was no answer. Then little Shill did something that Joanne will never forget. She came over to Joanne who was sitting cross legged on the floor and lay down in her lap and went to sleep. Luckily, she was a light calf because after only a few minutes Joanne's legs were going to sleep and were full of pins and needles, but she wasn't going to move as she didn't want to disturb the sleeping calf. This was the start of a lifelong friendship. Joanne stayed like that for as long as she could and could barely move at all by the time Shill woke up. Joanne knew that little Shill would need a friend for company and so she moved Sirris who was Shilling's sister and little Shills' aunty into the paddock and Sirris and Shill took to each other like ducks to water.

In spite of never having had a calf of her own, Sirris mothered the little brindle calf as if she was hers. It was Sirris' finest moment, as if she had lived her whole life to take care of her sister's baby. When it rained she licked her dry, when she was hungry she let her suck her teats (even though she had no milk, and Joanne gave Shill a big bottle of milk twice per day), and even when the calf ran around the paddock playing, old Sirris did her best to keep up. Between aunty Sirris and Joanne, little Shill had all the love and care that a calf could want, even though she had lost her mum at only 6 weeks of age.

CHAPTER 10

The Curly Cow

Young Shill grew into a lovely heifer, and then around the age of 4 months something happened that Joanne wasn't expecting. Shill began to grow horns.

At first, they were only little nubs on the side of her head, but as Shill got older they developed into a beautiful set of pointy horns that pointed forwards and turned up on the ends. Joanne often thought about decorating them in the same way that you see some of the cows in India, but never did. She thought Shill probably wouldn't like it, and didn't want to upset her.

The horn gene came from both the jersey and wagyu sides of the family and the final size and shape of them was a combination of both influences. Shill got the right one caught in

something in the paddock once, and popped the outer covering off which made one horn a bit shorter than the other. Joanne looked for that horn all over the paddock but never did manage to find it.

As she aged, Shills' horns started to thicken and curl which left Joanne worried that they might grow into the side of her head, but they just curled very close to Shills' eyes and came back around again. They became very thick and solid and ended up being quite spectacular. People often commented on them when they came to inspect the other cattle. Joanne still uses a skinny hair brush to scratch Shills' head under her curly horns because it's impossible for Shill to scratch there.

And so, Zenith Shill became the Curly Cow, she has had

14 calves of her own and still lives on the farm with Joanne who gives her a brush nearly every day. If Joanne is riding past on the quad and Shill wants a brush, she swings her head and licks her shoulder, as if to say, "I'm itchy mum, come and brush me." When Joanne is brushing her, if Shill has a spot

that is still itchy she licks it to show Joanne where to brush, and looks quite a sight when she lifts one back leg so that Joanne can brush between her udder and back leg.

Despite being a small, slightly built cow, Shill is the boss of the herd, and the other cows learnt at an early age that Shills little pointy horns were not to be messed with. Shill is 19 years old now, but still spritely. She will live out her days with Joanne on their farm, just like her mother, aunty and grandmother.

THE END

www.ingramcontent.com/pod-product-compliance
Lightning Source LLC
Chambersburg PA
CBHW041429270326
41933CB00023B/3490

* 9 7 8 1 9 2 5 2 3 0 3 6 9 *